Chemicals in Action

ELEMENTS AND COMPOUNDS

Chris Oxlade

REVISED AND UPDATED

Heinemann Library

Chicago, Illinois

© 2002, 2007 Heinemann Library
an imprint of Capstone Global Library, LLC
Chicago, Illinois

Customer Service 888-454-2279
Visit our website at www.heinemannraintree.com

Editorial: Clare Lewis
Design: Steve Mead and Fiona MacColl
Picture Research: Hannah Taylor
Production: Julie Carter
Originated by Modern Age
Printed in the United States of America in Eau Claire, Wisconsin. 052013   007416R

15 14 13
10 9 8 7 6 5 4 3

New edition ISBN: 978-1-4329-0052-6 (hardcover)
                  978-1-4329-0059-5 (paperback)

The Library of Congress has cataloged the first edition as follows:
Oxlade, Chris
    Elements and compounds / Chris Oxlade.
        p. cm. -- (Chemicals in Action)
    Includes bibliographical references and index.
    ISBN 1-58810-196-7
    1.   Chemical elements--Juvenile literature. 2. Chemicals—Juvenile
    literature[1. Chemical elements. 2. Chemicals] I. Title.
QD466 .O95 2001
546'.8—dc21
                                2001000103

Acknowledgments
The author and publishers are grateful to the following for permission to reproduce copyright material: Alamy p. 20, Andrew Lambert pp. **9**, **11**, **29**, Anthony Blake (Sue Atkinson) p. **34**, Corbis pp. **23**, **26**, Culture Archive p. **33**, Robert Harding p. **35**, Science Photo Library pp. **4**, **5**, **6**, **7**, **19**, **21**, **23** (bottom), **24**, **25**, **30**, **32**, **36**, **38**, Telegraph Colour Library pp. **12**, **13**, **18**, **22**, Trevor Clifford pp. **15**, **17**, **27**, **29**, **31**, **37**, **39**.

Cover photograph: computer model of part of a molecule, reproduced with permission of Science Photo Library.

The publishers would like to thank Ted Dolter and Dr. Nigel Saunders for their assistance in the preparation of this title.

Some words are shown in bold, **like this**. You can find out what they mean by looking in the glossary.

CONTENTS

CHEMICALS IN ACTION

What's the link between the Sun, an X-ray of a stomach, beautifully colored fireworks, and the ink in your pen? The answer is **elements** and **compounds**. All substances are made of elements and compounds, or a mixture of the two. Our knowledge of the different elements and compounds is used in making chemicals, in medical research, and in engineering.

The study of elements and compounds is part of the science of chemistry. Many people think of chemistry as something that scientists study by doing experiments in laboratories with special equipment. This part of chemistry is very important. It is how scientists find out what substances are made from and how they make new materials, but this is only a small part of chemistry. Most chemistry happens away from laboratories, in factories and chemical plants. It is used to manufacture a wide range of items, such as synthetic fibers for fabrics, drugs to treat diseases, explosives for fireworks, **solvents** for paints, and fertilizers for growing crops.

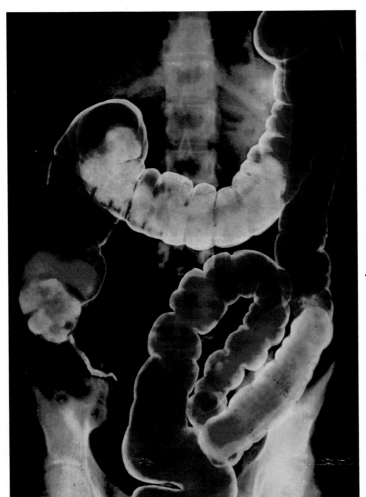

The shape of this patient's large intestine (colon) shows up on an X-ray because he or she has just eaten a meal containing the element barium.

About the experiments

There are several experiments for you to try. Doing these experiments will help you understand some of the chemistry in this book. An experiment is designed to help solve a scientific problem. Scientists use a logical approach to experiments so they can make conclusions from the results of the experiments. A scientist first writes down a hypothesis, which might be the answer to the problem, then designs an experiment to test the hypothesis. He or she writes down the results of the experiment and concludes whether or not the results show that the hypothesis is true. We only know what we do about chemistry because scientists have carefully carried out thousands of experiments over hundreds of years.

Experiments have allowed scientists to discover all of the hundred or more elements we know about. They have also learned how these elements combine to make compounds, and even how to make new elements.

DOING THE EXPERIMENTS

All the experiments in this book have been designed for you to do at home with everyday substances and equipment. They can also be done in your school's science class. Always follow the safety advice given with each experiment. Ask an adult to help you when the instructions tell you to.

The rockets on this space shuttle are filled with chemicals. They combine together to release the energy that lifts the shuttle off the ground.

ELEMENTS, COMPOUNDS, AND MIXTURES

Every substance on Earth (and Earth itself!) is made up of tiny **particles** called **atoms**. Scientists have found 90 different types of atom that occur naturally on Earth, and they have made a few more under special conditions in the laboratory. Atoms make up substances called elements, compounds, and **mixtures**.

An element is a substance made up of just one type of atom. For example, oxygen is an element because it contains only oxygen atoms. An element is the most simple type of substance there is.

The scene near the top of a volcano. The yellow areas are crystals of the element sulfur.

A compound is a substance made up of different elements joined together. For example, water is a compound made up of the elements oxygen and hydrogen. The atoms of these two elements are joined together to form water. These connections are called chemical **bonds**. Compounds can be separated into simpler substances, such as elements or simpler compounds, by breaking these chemical bonds.

Building with elements

You can think of elements as colored building blocks. Each element would be represented by a block with a **unique** color, different to the blocks representing the other elements. A compound would contain blocks of different colors joined together.

By combining any two colors, or three colors, or more, you could build millions of different compounds. So you can see that although there are only a hundred or so different elements on Earth, they can combine to make millions of different compounds. Each different compound also contains a specific proportion of elements. For example, water always contains two parts hydrogen and one part oxygen.

Mixtures

In science, a mixture is a substance that contains different elements and compounds that are *not* joined together by chemical bonds. A mixture of two different elements is not a compound because the elements are not joined by bonds. The air that you breathe is an example of a mixture. It contains some elements, such as oxygen and nitrogen, and some compounds, such as carbon dioxide. A mixture can always be separated into the individual substances it contains.

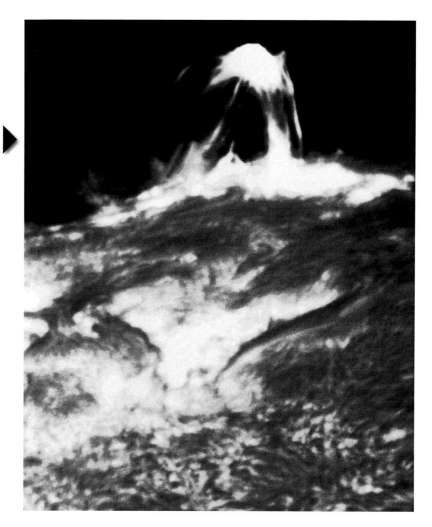

All the stars (including our Sun), the planets, and moons in the Universe are made of the same elements and compounds as the ones found on Earth. This solar flare erupting from the Sun's surface contains elements that can also be found on Earth.

Atoms and molecules

All substances, whether they are elements, compounds, or mixtures, are made up of tiny particles. These particles are either individual atoms, or groups of atoms called **molecules**. An atom is the smallest particle of an element that can exist. Imagine breaking a piece of iron into smaller and smaller pieces. Eventually you would end up with individual atoms. These would still be the element iron—but if you broke the atom into pieces (which would be extremely difficult) those pieces would no longer be iron.

Atoms are incredibly small. Even big ones are less than a few billionths of an inch across. They are so small that the period at the end of this sentence contains millions and millions of atoms of the elements that make up the ink.

Molecules

A molecule is a particle made up of two or more atoms joined to each other with chemical bonds. The simplest molecules are made up of two atoms of the same element. For example, the gas oxygen is made up of oxygen molecules, and each of these molecules is made up of two oxygen atoms joined together. The **symbol** for the element oxygen is O, but the **formula** for oxygen gas is O_2, to show that it is made up of molecules with two oxygen atoms. The molecules of some substances, such as plastics, contain thousands of atoms.

INSIDE AN ATOM

Atoms are made up of even smaller particles called **protons**, **neutrons**, and **electrons**. These are called sub-atomic particles. At the center of every atom is a nucleus, made up of protons and neutrons joined together in a group. Electrons travel around the nucleus.

An atom of helium ▶

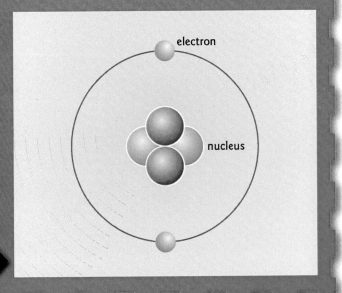

electron

nucleus

ELEMENTS, A COMPOUND AND A MIXTURE

1 Iron (a gray **metal**) and sulfur (a solid, yellow **nonmetal**) are both elements. This is a mixture of iron filings and sulfur powder. The iron and sulfur are not chemically combined. They can be separated with a magnet, which picks up only the iron.

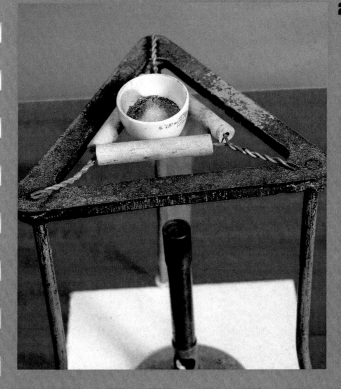

2 If a mixture of iron filings and sulfur powder is heated, a **chemical reaction** starts. It continues until the iron and sulfur are joined together. A gray solid is left. This is iron sulfide, which is a compound. It is made up of the same elements as the original mixture, but now the elements are joined by chemical bonds. The iron cannot be separated using a magnet.

CLASSIFYING ELEMENTS

Every element has a name and a symbol. The symbol is an abbreviation (a shortened version) of the element's name. It is used to represent the element in chemical formulas and equations. For example, the chemical symbol for the element carbon is C. The symbols of elements do not always seem to match the elements' names, however. This is because the symbols come from different languages. For example, the symbol for iron is Fe, which comes from *ferrum*, the Latin word for iron.

The periodic table

The periodic table is a list of all known elements. The elements are arranged so that elements with similar **properties** are close together. For example, fluorine (F) and chlorine (Cl) are gases that react very easily with other elements, so they are close together in the table. The periodic table gets its name from the fact that the elements' properties repeat themselves every few elements, or periodically. A chemist can tell what the properties of an element are likely to be by looking at its position in the table.

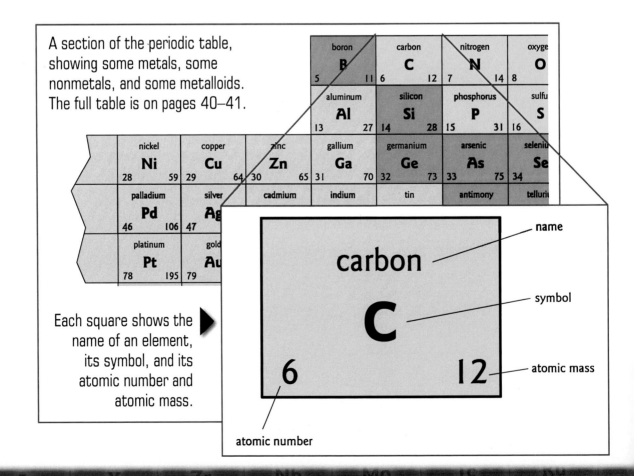

A section of the periodic table, showing some metals, some nonmetals, and some metalloids. The full table is on pages 40–41.

boron	carbon	nitrogen	oxyge
B	C	N	O
5 11	6 12	7 14	8
aluminum	silicon	phosphorus	sulfu
Al	Si	P	S
13 27	14 28	15 31	16

nickel	copper	zinc	gallium	germanium	arsenic	seleniu
Ni	Cu	Zn	Ga	Ge	As	Se
28 59	29 64	30 65	31 70	32 73	33 75	34
palladium	silver	cadmium	indium	tin	antimony	telluri
Pd	Ag					
46 106	47					
platinum	gold					
Pt	Au					
78 195	79					

Each square shows the name of an element, its symbol, and its atomic number and atomic mass.

name

carbon

symbol

C

6   12

atomic mass

atomic number

Chlorine (rear), bromine, and iodine (front) have similar chemical properties. They are all members of group 17 of the periodic table.

Groups and periods

The vertical columns of elements are called groups. The horizontal rows of elements are called periods. The table also shows which elements are metals, which are nonmetals, and which are **metalloids** (you can find out more about these on page 13). Some groups have special names:

Group 1: The **alkali** metals
Group 2: The alkaline earth metals
Group 17: The halogens
Group 18: The noble gases

INVENTING A TABLE

In 1829 German chemist Johann Wolfgang Döbereiner (1780–1849) noticed that some elements could be put into groups of three, each with similar properties. He called these groups triads. In 1864 English chemist John Newlands (1837–1898) arranged the elements that were known at the time into order of the masses of their atoms. He found that each element had properties like the element eight places in front of it, so he called this his Law of Octaves (because it was like eight musical notes in an octave). In 1868 Russian chemist Dimitri Mendeleyev (1834–1907) spotted more patterns in the behavior of the elements that had been discovered by that time. He drew up the first periodic table that showed elements with similar properties in columns.

Metals and nonmetals

The elements in the periodic table are divided into two main groups. They are the metals and the nonmetals. Roughly three-quarters of the elements are metals, and these appear on the left side of the periodic table. The nonmetals appear on the right side.

The properties of metals

All metals look shiny. Sometimes the shine on the surface of a piece of metal gradually disappears as the metal reacts with oxygen in the air. The shine comes back if the metal is polished, and if it is cut open the metal that is revealed is also shiny. Most metals are very hard, but a few are so soft that you can cut into them with a knife. Metals are also malleable, which means they can be bent or beaten into different shapes without breaking.

All metals are solids at room temperature except mercury, which is a liquid. This is because metals have high **melting points**. For example, the melting point of iron is 1,535 °C (2,795 °F). Metals also have high **boiling points**. Iron boils at 2,861 °C (5,182 °F). All metals let heat and electricity pass through them easily, so they can be described as good **conductors** of heat and electricity. Only a very few metals are magnetic, which means they are attracted by magnets. Iron is a magnetic metal.

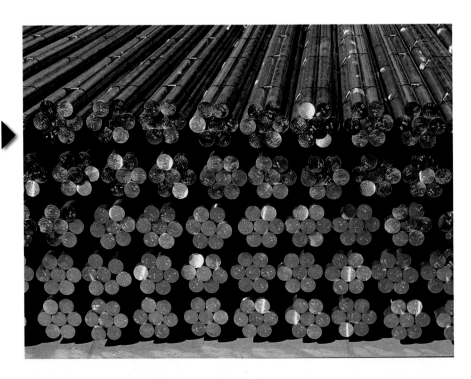

Copper is an extremely good conductor of electricity. These copper rods will be made into copper wire for cables.

The properties of nonmetals

All metals share similar properties. Nonmetals, however, have a wide range of different properties. For example, they come in several different colors. At room temperature most nonmetals are gases, some are solids, and one (bromine) is a liquid. This is because nonmetals have a wide range of melting and boiling points. For example, sulfur is a solid at room temperature because its melting point is 113 °C (235 °F), and nitrogen is a gas at room temperature because its boiling point is -196 °C (-321 °F). Nonmetals are not good conductors of electricity or heat. Carbon is an exception because it conducts electricity just as well as metal. No nonmetals are magnetic.

Metalloids

A few elements, such as silicon, have some of the properties of metals and some of the properties of nonmetals. They are not really metals and not really nonmetals, so they are called metalloids or semi-metals.

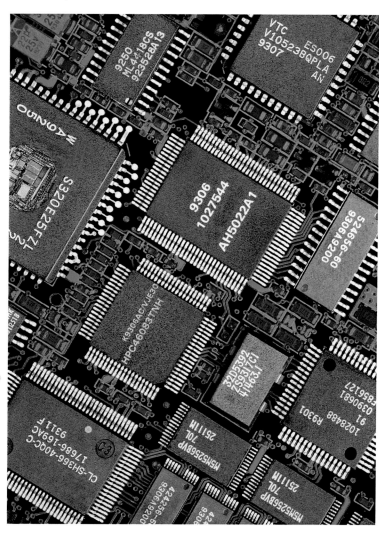

Their most important use is in making materials called semiconductors. A semiconductor is a material that can conduct some electricity better than an **insulator**, but not as much or as well as metals can. Semiconductors are used in electronic components and microchips.

Microchips on a complex circuit board. The semiconductor chips themselves are encased in protective plastic.

Metals in reactions

Some metals react very well with common chemicals, such as **acids**, the air, and water. Other metals do not react with chemicals at all. The **reactivity series** (see below) is a list of common metals in order of how well they react, or how reactive they are.

Metals at the top of the series, such as potassium and sodium, are extremely reactive. These metals are found in group 1 of the periodic table. They react quickly with the air to make metal **oxides,** so they have to be stored in oil to keep the air away from them. They fizz strongly when they are put in water, and react violently when they are placed in acid. These reactions make hydrogen gas and lots of heat. The heat ignites the hydrogen, making it explode.

Metals at the bottom of the reactivity series, such as gold and silver, are not reactive at all. They do not even react with strong acids, such as hydrochloric acid. These unreactive metals all come from the large block in the center of the periodic table called the transition metals.

The reactivity series of common metals. It shows, for example, that aluminum is more reactive than zinc, but less reactive than magnesium.

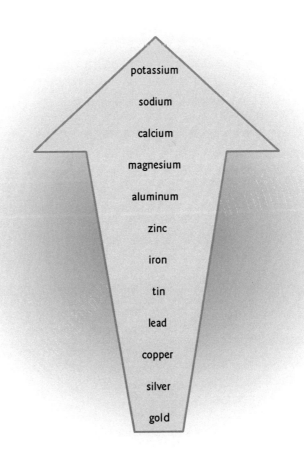

potassium

sodium

calcium

magnesium

aluminum

zinc

iron

tin

lead

copper

silver

gold

EXPERIMENT: REACTIVE METALS

Problem

Which common metals are most reactive?

Hypothesis

To find which metals are most reactive, we can put pieces of the metals in a weak acid and watch what happens. The one that fizzes most quickly will be the most reactive.

EQUIPMENT

- nail or screw made of iron or steel
- galvanized (zinc-coated) nail or screw
- nail or screw made of copper or brass
- white vinegar (colored vinegar will work)
- three small jars
- one bowl

Experiment steps

1 Put a nail or screw into each of the three small jars. Pour just enough vinegar into the jars to cover the nails or screws. Watch what happens over a few minutes. While you are waiting, ask an adult to heat some water (it does not need to boil).

2 Make sure a window is open because the next part gets really smelly! Ask the adult to pour some hot water into the bowl. Carefully put your jars into the water so that the hot water will heat up the vinegar in the jars. Again, watch what happens over a few minutes. Be sure not to breathe deeply near the warm vinegar.

3 Make notes of your results. If bubbles are coming off the surface of the metal, there is a reaction happening. You can make sure by gently swirling the vinegar to remove any bubbles. Then watch to see if they start coming off on their own again. Write down whether the reaction is fast, steady, or slow, or whether there is no reaction at all.

4 Write down the three metals in order of their speeds of reaction, starting your list with the most reactive and working down to the least reactive. This is your reactivity series.

Results

Write down the three metals in order of their speeds of reaction. This is your reactivity series. Which metal is the most reactive? Which is the least reactive. You can check your results on page 47.

ELEMENTS ON EARTH

There are 90 elements that occur naturally on Earth. They are found in the rocks that make up Earth's crust, in fresh water and sea water, in the air that makes up Earth's atmosphere, and in animals and plants.

There are different amounts of each element on Earth. Some elements, such as oxygen and carbon, are found in large amounts and are easy to find. These are "abundant" elements. Many elements are only found in very tiny amounts. Some elements occur naturally, uncombined with other elements, normally as part of a mixture. Gold, for example, is found in the ground, and oxygen is in the air. However, most elements are trapped in compounds.

Extracting elements

We use nearly all of the elements for one job or another in industry, medicine, agriculture, and science. Before we can use them, we have to **extract** them from where they are found. This involves collecting the mixtures or compounds the elements are in, and then breaking them up to remove the elements. Many different chemical processes and physical processes are used to do this.

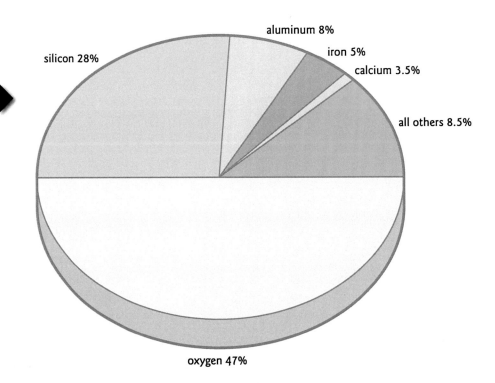

A pie chart of the most common elements in Earth's crust. The element oxygen is the most common element found in Earth's crust. All living things need this vital element to survive.

silicon 28%
aluminum 8%
iron 5%
calcium 3.5%
all others 8.5%
oxygen 47%

EXPERIMENT: CHLORINE FROM SALT WATER

Problem Where can we get chlorine from?

Hypothesis Chlorine is one of the elements in common salt, and sea water contains lots of dissolved common salt. So it may be possible to get chlorine by **electrolysis** of salt water.

EQUIPMENT
- pencil or mechanical pencil leads
- clothes pin
- aluminum foil
- battery
- table salt
- glass jar

Experiment steps

1 Pour water into the jar until it is 1 inch (2 centimeters) below the rim. Stir in, and dissolve, one or two teaspoons of salt.

2 Wrap some aluminum foil around one of the jaws of the clothes pin. Slip the clothes pin over the rim of the jar so that the jaw with the foil is on the inside. Use the pin to clamp two pencil leads to the inside of the jar (the clothes pin should be above the salt **solution** and the leads should be in it). Another way is to sharpen a pencil at both ends and clamp this with the clothes pin (put the top end of the pencil lead in contact with the foil). Cut a strip of aluminum foil about 8 inches (20 centimeters) long and 1 inch (2 centimeters) wide, wrap one end of this around the foil on the jaw but leave about 6 inches (15 centimeters) free at the other end.

3 Cut a strip of aluminum foil about 12 inches (30 centimeters) long and 1 inch (2 centimeters) wide. Push one end of the foil into the salt solution at the opposite end to the clothes pin, bend it over the rim of the jar, and pass it underneath.

4 Connect the positive (+) terminal of the battery to the foil running from the clothes pin, and connect the negative (-) terminal of the battery to the other piece of foil. Watch what happens.

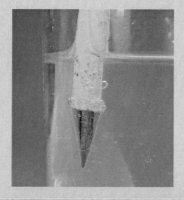

5 Tiny bubbles of gas form at each **electrode**. Smell (but not too closely) the gas coming from the pencil lead.

Results

Do you recognize the smell of the gas? What kind of gas do you think it is? You can check your results on page 47.

Common metals

Metals are extracted from rocks in Earth's crust. The rocks contain minerals called **ores**. An ore is a compound made up of a metal combined with other elements. The metals that we use most are the ones that have plenty of ores and are easiest to extract from their ores.

Metals are often mixed with each other, or with nonmetals, to make materials called **alloys**. Alloys have more useful properties than the metals they are made from.

Iron

Iron is the most widely used metal. It is hard and gray, and the most common magnetic metal. Some iron is made into iron objects such as gates and railings, but most iron is made into steel. Steel is an alloy.

It contains about 99 percent iron and about 1 percent carbon. Steel is made into cars, ships, buildings, and hundreds of other objects. Iron's biggest problem is that it rusts quickly in damp air. Rusting is a reaction of the iron with oxygen and water. Rust eats away iron or steel, making the metal weak.

◄ All modern high-rise buildings have a super-strong skeleton made of steel or concrete reinforced with steel.

Copper

Copper is a soft, brown metal that is easy to shape and cut. Copper is a very good conductor of electricity, so it is used to make wires and cables. It is also made into pipes for water supply and heating systems. Copper is mixed with zinc to make an alloy called brass. Brass does not lose its shine and is harder than copper or zinc.

Aluminum

Aluminum is a silver-colored metal that has a low **density**. Most aluminum is made into soda cans, pans, and aluminum foil. The aluminum on the surface of an aluminum object slowly reacts with the air to form aluminum oxide. This forms a layer that protects the aluminum underneath.

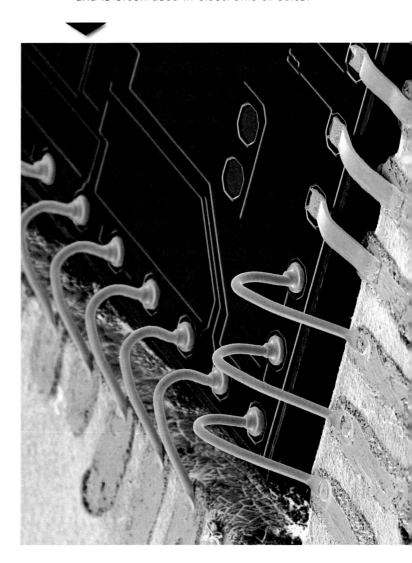

Gold conducts electricity extremely well and is often used in electronic circuits.

DISCOVERING METALS

The metals we know about today were discovered gradually over thousands of years. Most were discovered in the last 200 years. Gold and silver were discovered more than 5,000 years ago. This is because they are at the bottom of the reactivity series—they do not react with other elements to form compounds and so are easy to find as elements. Copper was discovered next. Copper is only slightly reactive and is released from its ore when the ore is heated. It was probably discovered by accident, when a piece of ore was heated in a fire.

Common nonmetals

Nonmetal elements come from the air in the atmosphere, from sea water, and from ores in rocks, like metals do. Many of the nonmetals that are gases at room temperature, such as nitrogen and oxygen, can be found in the air. They are extracted by **fractional distillation** of the air.

Hydrogen

Hydrogen is the simplest of all the elements. It is also the most common element in the Universe. Each hydrogen atom is made up of one proton and one electron. At room temperature, hydrogen is a colorless, odorless gas that is very explosive. Hydrogen is used to make many different chemicals, including fertilizers. It is extracted from natural gas.

Hydrogen is used as a fuel in fuel cells. Fuel cells are like batteries, but have a continuous supply of **reactants**. They can be used to power cars.

Carbon

Carbon is an unusual and important element. It is found in two very different forms, diamond and graphite. Graphite is the substance that pencil leads are made from, and it is the only nonmetal substance that conducts electricity. Diamond is used in jewelry and in the blades of cutting tools because it is extremely hard. Both diamond and graphite have melting points higher than most metals. The differences between diamond and graphite are caused by the carbon atoms being joined together in different ways. Carbon is the most important element for life and most of the compounds that make up animals and plants contain carbon. These are called **organic** compounds. You can find out more about them on page 32.

Nitrogen

Nitrogen is a colorless, odorless gas that makes up 78 percent of the air in the atmosphere. Nitrogen is vital for plants because it is needed to build the compounds that make up plant **cells**. In industry nitrogen is made by fractional distillation of air. It is used to make a compound called ammonia, as well as nitric **acid**. These can be used to make fertilizers and explosives.

The drilling tip of a dentist's drill is coated with particles of diamond, a form of carbon.

Phosphorus

The element phosphorus is a solid that occurs in two common forms— white and red. White phosphorus is waxy, poisonous, and very reactive. It has to be stored under water because it catches fire in the air. Red phosphorus is used to make matches and distress flares.

FRACTIONAL DISTILLATION

Fractional distillation is a process that is used to separate a mixture of liquids. It is the process used to extract gases from air, which itself is a mixture of gases. First, the air is cooled until it **condenses** to become a liquid. Then, it is warmed up again gradually. Each gas in the mixture has a different boiling point. As the temperature of the liquid reaches the boiling point of one of the gases, then that gas boils and is collected. Then the temperature is raised again and the next gas boils and is collected.

More nonmetals

On these pages you can find out about more nonmetal elements. They include the elements in group 17 of the periodic table, called the halogens, and group 18 of the periodic table, called the noble gases.

Oxygen

Oxygen is a colorless, odorless gas that makes up 21 percent of the air. Oxygen is the part of the air that we use when we breathe, so it is vital for life. Many substances react with oxygen when they are left in the open air. For example, burning is a reaction between a substance and oxygen in the air. This normally only happens if the substance is heated. Oxygen is extracted from the air by fractional distillation. It is also the most common element in the rocks of Earth's crust.

A major use of noble gases is in the bulbs of illuminated signs.

Normal oxygen molecules contain two oxygen atoms, but high in the atmosphere, oxygen is found as a gas called ozone. Each molecule of ozone is made up of three oxygen atoms.

Sulfur

Sulfur is a yellow solid. It is found as an element in rocks, especially in areas of the world where there are volcanoes. You often see it on the surface around hot springs. Sulfur is used in the manufacture of sulfuric acid. It is also added to rubber in vehicle tires to make the rubber last longer.

The noble gases

The elements in group 18 of the periodic table are nonmetal gases called the noble gases. They are all completely unreactive, and do not react with other elements to make compounds. Most noble gases are found in tiny amounts in the air, and are extracted by fractional distillation. Helium is extracted from natural gas by fractional distillation.

The halogens

The elements in group 17 of the periodic table are called the halogens. They include fluorine, chlorine, bromine, and iodine. Fluorine is made into compounds used for non-stick coatings. Chlorine is used as a disinfectant because it kills **microorganisms**. For example, small amounts of chlorine are dissolved in swimming pool water to kill bacteria that might spread disease from one swimmer to another. Fluorine and chlorine are very reactive. They are also poisonous in high concentrations when they are elements, but not when they are in compounds. Bromine is a brown liquid that gives off poisonous bromine gas. Iodine is a dark purple solid. It is important in our diets and is also used as an antiseptic.

Many types of light bulbs, including those used in car head-lights, are filled with halogen gases.

JOSEPH PRIESTLEY (1733–1804)

Joseph Priestley was a minister, English teacher, and chemist. He studied how gases were formed during chemical reactions. He discovered nitrogen in 1772 and oxygen in 1774. He found oxygen by heating mercury oxide, which divided into mercury and oxygen.

COMPOUNDS

A compound is a substance that is made up of different elements. The atoms of the elements are joined together by chemical bonds. Some compounds are very simple and might contain two or three different elements joined together in a simple way. For example, sodium chloride (common salt) is made up of just sodium and chlorine. A piece of salt contains one chlorine atom for every sodium atom. Its formula is NaCl. Other compounds are very complicated. They might contain several different elements joined together in different amounts. For example, the compound glucose, which is a type of sugar, is made up of carbon, hydrogen, and oxygen. It contains one oxygen atom and two hydrogen atoms for every carbon atom. Its formula is $C_6H_{12}O_6$.

Making compounds

Compounds are made when different elements join together in chemical reactions. For example, when the element carbon burns, it combines with the element oxygen, from the air, to make the compound carbon dioxide.

carbon	+	oxygen	$\rightarrow$	carbon dioxide
C	+	O_2	$\rightarrow$	CO_2

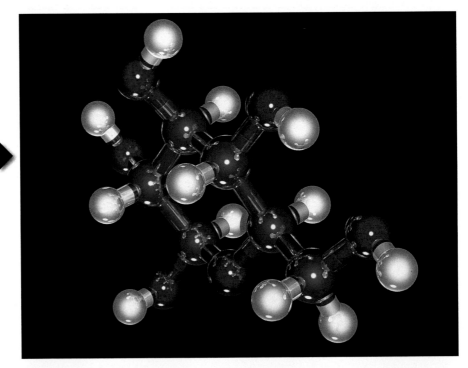

A model of a molecule of glucose ($C_6H_{12}O_6$).

Molecules and giant structures

Some compounds are made up of molecules. Remember that a molecule is a particle made up of atoms joined to each other. All the molecules in a compound are identical, and they each contain one or more atoms of each element in the compound. For example, carbon dioxide is made up of molecules. Every molecule of carbon dioxide is made of one carbon atom joined to two oxygen atoms.

Some compounds are not made up of molecules. Instead, each atom joins to all the atoms around it. The atoms join together to make a structure called a **lattice**. The atoms in a lattice often turn into particles called **ions**. They do this by losing or gaining electrons. For example, sodium chloride is made of sodium ions and chlorine ions arranged in a lattice. Each sodium atom loses an electron and each chlorine atom gains one.

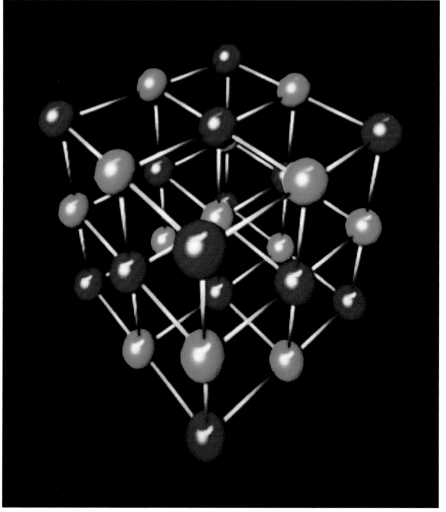

This computer graphic shows a model of part of a giant ionic lattice of sodium chloride. Sodium ions (in red) and chloride ions (in green) repeat themselves to create the lattice.

Ca
Sc
Ti
51 24
52 25
55 26
56 27
20
40 21
45 22
48 23
molybdenum
technetium
ruthenium
rhodium
strontium
yttrium
zirconium
niobium

Families of compounds

Simple compounds come in two main groups. One group includes compounds that contain a metal element combined with one or more nonmetal elements. Examples of these compounds are iron sulfide (made up of the metal iron and the nonmetal sulfur) and copper sulfate (made up of the metal copper and the nonmetals sulfur and oxygen). The other group includes compounds that contain two or more nonmetal elements combined together. Examples of these compounds are carbon dioxide (made up of the nonmetals carbon and oxygen) and hydrogen chloride (made up of the nonmetals hydrogen and chlorine). There are no compounds made up of metals combined with metals.

More families

Compounds are also put into groups or families because of the elements they contain. An oxide is a compound that contains a metal or a nonmetal combined with oxygen. Aluminum oxide and carbon dioxide are examples of oxides. A carbonate is a compound that contains a metal combined with carbon and oxygen, such as magnesium carbonate. Sulfates and nitrates are similar to carbonates, but they contain sulfur or nitrogen instead of carbon.

A salt is a compound made when an acid reacts with a **base**. A base is often a metal oxide, and when a base dissolves in water it makes an alkali. A salt always contains a metal and a nonmetal. Copper sulfate and sodium chloride are examples of salts.

◀ These limestone cliffs are made up of calcium, carbon, and oxygen in the form of calcium carbonate.

EXPERIMENT: MAKING A METAL OXIDE

Problem

How can we make a metal oxide?

Hypothesis

Oxides are formed in a reaction between a substance and oxygen in the air. Heating a metal in the air should make an oxide.

EQUIPMENT
- aluminum foil
- kitchen tongs or wooden clothes pin
- old plate

Experiment steps

1 Tear a piece of aluminum foil about 12 inches (30 centimeters) long and ½ to 1 inch (1 to 2 centimeters) wide. Hold one end in a pair of tongs or wooden clothes pin.

2 An adult must do this step with you. Heat the last ½ inch (1 centimeter) of the foil in the flame of a gas stove for a few seconds and then remove it. Watch what happens.

3 Allow the aluminum to cool. Crumble the burned aluminum onto the plate. Can you see a gray powder?

Results

What do you see when you crumble the burned aluminum? What do you think this substance is? You can check your results on page 47.

Compound names and formulas

You know that each element has a name and a symbol that is used to represent the element in chemical equations. Compounds also have names and formulas. The name of a compound contains the names of the elements that are in it. For example, iron oxide is a compound that contains the elements iron and oxygen, and sodium chloride is a compound that contains sodium and chlorine. Unfortunately, the compound names are not always easy to understand. Some compounds have common names, such as water, that do not tell you what elements the compounds contain.

Some compound names also tell you how many atoms of each element are in the compounds. For example, the "mono" part of the name carbon monoxide tells you that the compound contains one oxygen atom for every carbon atom. Carbon and oxygen also form the compound carbon dioxide. The "di" shows that carbon dioxide contains two oxygen atoms for every carbon atom.

Name endings

Compound names always end with letters such as "ide" and "ate." The letters "ide" mean that the compound contains two elements only. For example, copper oxide contains copper and oxygen only. The letters "ate" mean that the compound contains oxygen as well. For example, calcium phosphate contains calcium, phosphorus, and oxygen.

Compound formulas

Every compound has a formula made up of symbols (for elements) and numbers. The formula tells you what elements are in the compound and how many atoms of each element combine to make up the compound. Here are some examples of compound names, their formulas, and the number of atoms of each element that combine to make up the compound:

Compound name	Formulas	Number of atoms of each element
carbon monoxide	CO	1 x C; 1 x O
carbon dioxide	CO_2	1 x C; 2 x O
calcium carbonate	$CaCO_3$	1 x Ca; 1 x C; 3 x O
calcium hydroxide	$Ca(OH)_2$	1 x Ca; 2 x O; 2 x H

In chemical equations you often see a number before the formula of a compound. This means that more than one molecule of the compound takes part in the equation. For example, H_2O is the formula for water, and $2H_2O$ means two molecules of water, each containing two hydrogen atoms and one oxygen atom.

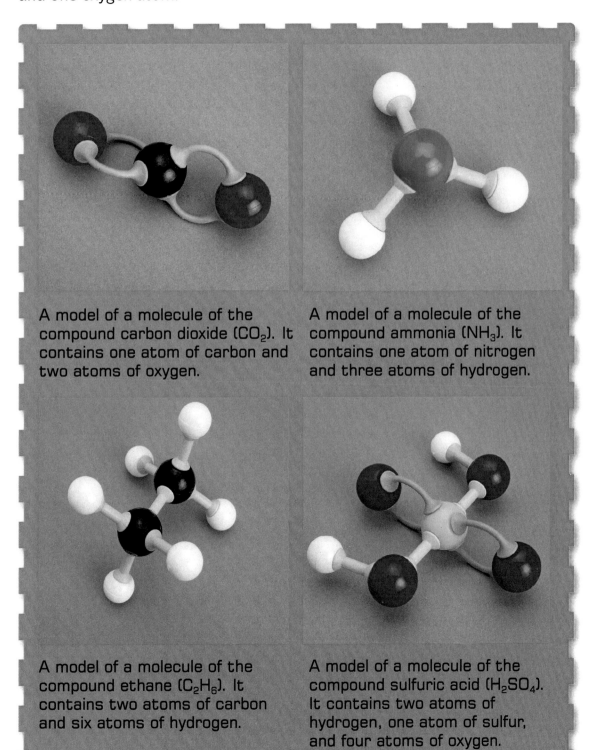

A model of a molecule of the compound carbon dioxide (CO_2). It contains one atom of carbon and two atoms of oxygen.

A model of a molecule of the compound ammonia (NH_3). It contains one atom of nitrogen and three atoms of hydrogen.

A model of a molecule of the compound ethane (C_2H_6). It contains two atoms of carbon and six atoms of hydrogen.

A model of a molecule of the compound sulfuric acid (H_2SO_4). It contains two atoms of hydrogen, one atom of sulfur, and four atoms of oxygen.

Physical properties

The physical properties of an element or compound include its color, texture, density, and its melting and boiling points. Different elements have different physical properties, and so do different compounds. Compounds also have very different properties to the elements they are made from. Some physical properties depend on how strongly the particles that make up the element or compound are joined together.

Melting and boiling points

Melting is turning something from solid to liquid. It happens when a solid is hot enough for the bonds between the particles in the solid to begin to break, allowing the particles to move around. Boiling is turning something from liquid to gas. It happens when a liquid is hot enough for the bonds between its particles to break completely, allowing the particles to escape and form a gas.

Metallic elements have strong bonds between their atoms, and compounds made up of ions have strong bonds between their ions. They have high melting points and boiling points because the temperature must be very high before the bonds between the atoms or ions will break. This is why most metals, and **ionic compounds**, such as sodium chloride, are solids at room temperature.

This is not ice, but solid carbon dioxide. Carbon dioxide has very low melting and boiling points, so it turns straight from a solid to a gas at room temperature.

Elements and compounds that are made up of simple molecules are different. There are strong bonds between the atoms that make up the molecules, but weaker bonds between one molecule and the next. These elements and compounds have low melting and boiling points. This is why most compounds made of simple molecules are liquids or gases at room temperature.

ELEMENTS FROM COMPOUNDS

1 The red solid in this test tube is mercury oxide. It is a compound of mercury and oxygen.

When the solid is heated it gradually begins to change. Shiny, liquid mercury begins to appear.

2 Eventually all of the solid is gone and only mercury is left. The oxygen, which is a gas, has escaped into the air. You can see that the properties of the elements in a compound are very different to the properties of the compound they make.

This type of reaction is called a **decomposition** reaction.

| mercury oxide | → | mercury + oxygen |
| 2HgO | → | 2Hg + O$_2$ |

ORGANIC COMPOUNDS

Your body tissues, such as your skin and muscles, contain a large collection of complicated compounds—and so do the tissues of all animals and plants. These compounds are called organic compounds. Organic compounds are also found in fossil fuels, such as oil and gas, because these fuels were formed from the remains of animals and plants. Organic chemistry is the branch of chemistry that studies organic compounds.

Carbon chains

All organic compounds contain the element carbon. Carbon atoms have a special property—each one can attach with up to four other atoms. This means that carbon atoms can build up into very complex molecules of different shapes: long chains containing thousands of carbon atoms, chains with branches off of them, and even rings. The two other main elements in organic compounds are oxygen and hydrogen.

Models of molecules of the simple organic compounds methane (CH_4), ethane (C_2H_6), and propane (C_3H_8).

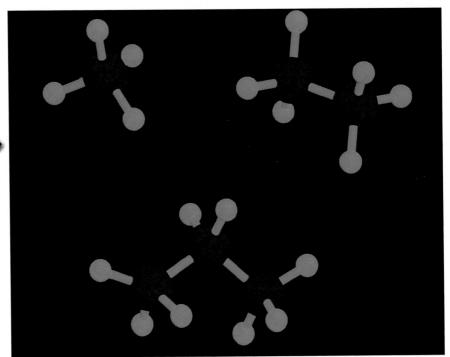

Compounds in living things

Animals and plants contain thousands of different organic compounds. Sugars, proteins, and fats are examples of these organic compounds. One of the simplest organic compounds in our bodies is a sugar called glucose. Its formula is $C_6H_{12}O_6$.

Glucose is made in plants during a process called **photosynthesis**. It is broken down in animals and plants during a process called **respiration**. During respiration, energy is released. Here is the equation for the reaction that happens during respiration:

$$\text{glucose} + \text{oxygen} \rightarrow \text{carbon dioxide} + \text{water}$$
$$C_6H_{12}O_6 + 6O_2 \rightarrow 6CO_2 + 6H_2O$$

The energy released is used in animals and plants for growth and movement, and to make other chemical reactions happen. Sugars such as glucose are examples of compounds called carbohydrates because they contain only carbon, hydrogen, and oxygen.

Proteins are very complex organic compounds. A protein molecule can contain many thousands of atoms. Proteins are the basic building blocks of **cells** and take part in many of the chemical reactions that make our bodies work. Fats are organic compounds that are stores of food for animals and plants. They are broken down into simpler substances that are used in respiration when the body needs energy.

Materials from oil

The fossil fuel petroleum is a mixture of many organic compounds. Some of these compounds are quite simple, such as ethane (C_2H_6). Others are very complicated, with molecules containing chains of 40 or more carbon atoms. Petroleum is separated into its parts by fractional distillation (see page 21). Some petroleum products, such as kerosene and butane, are used as fuels. Some are used as lubricants for machinery. Others are the raw materials that are used to make plastics.

This radio casing is made from bakelite (one of the first plastics) because it does not conduct electricity.

MIXTURES

A mixture is a substance made up of different elements and compounds. The elements and compounds are not joined with chemical bonds. Each element or compound in a mixture is called a constituent. A mixture can have constituents that are solids, liquids, or gases, or even all three together.

Mixtures of particles

Sometimes the particles in a mixture are individual atoms or molecules. For example, the air in the atmosphere is a mixture of molecules of different gases, such as nitrogen and oxygen. Sometimes the particles are clumps of atoms or molecules. For example, in a mixture of salt and granulated sugar, the particles are small crystals of salt and sugar. Each crystal contains millions of atoms. Sometimes a mixture contains individual atoms or molecules mixed with clumps of atoms or molecules. For example, smoke from a bonfire is a mixture of gas molecules and tiny specks of carbon, and muddy water is a mixture of water molecules and small pieces of rock.

This salad dressing is a mixture of tiny drops of oil and vinegar that slowly separate when the dressing is left to stand.

Pure gold is described as 24-carat gold. Gold used in jewelry is mixed with other metals to make it harder.

Solutions

A **solution** is also a mixture. A solution is formed when a solid, a liquid, or a gas dissolves in a liquid. For example, if you stir sugar into hot water, the sugar dissolves. It breaks up into individual sugar molecules. You end up with a solution that is a mixture of water molecules and sugar molecules. In a solution, the substance that dissolves (such as the sugar) is called the **solute** and the liquid it dissolves in (such as water) is called the **solvent**.

Pure substances

In chemistry a pure substance is one that contains only one element or compound. Many substances that seem to be pure are not really pure because they contain small amounts of other materials. They are actually mixtures, and the other materials in them are called impurities. For example, the water that comes out of your tap is not pure water. There are impurities, such as calcium hydrogencarbonate, dissolved in it. When the water is boiled, this forms calcium carbonate, which is left behind as scale in the boiling pot.

Separating mixtures

Because the parts of a mixture are not attached to each other with chemical bonds, a mixture can be separated into its constituents by physical processes. There are four main ways of separating mixtures and they are filtration, evaporation, distillation, and chromatography.

Separating mixtures

Chemists often need to separate mixtures into their different constituents. For example, they might need to extract a useful chemical from a mixture of chemicals, or they might want to purify a substance by removing the impurities from it. Alternatively, they might want to find out what substances are in a mixture.

Filtering

Filtering is used to separate a mixture of a liquid and an undissolved solid. The mixture is poured through filter paper, which has microscopic holes in it. The liquid can get through the holes but the solids cannot. For example, if you filter muddy water, the water molecules pass through the holes in the paper and can be collected in a beaker, but the particles of soil are trapped.

Chromatography

Chromatography is used to find out what the constituents of a mixture are. Scientists use chromatography to test whether substances are pure, or to find whether two mixtures contain the same constituents. The simplest type of chromatography is paper chromatography. A blob of a mixture, such as ink (which is a mixture of dyes), is put on a piece of filter paper. The end of the paper is then placed in a solvent such as water. The solvent moves through the paper, carrying the dyes with it. Different types of dye are carried different distances before they are left on the paper.

◀ A centrifuge is used to separate mixtures very quickly. As it spins at very high speed the most dense part of the mixture moves to the bottom of each tube.

EXPERIMENT: PAPER CHROMATOGRAPHY

Problem   How can we find out whether the ink two pens use is the same?

Hypothesis   We can use paper chromatography to find out what dyes are in the inks. If the dyes match, the inks are probably the same.

EQUIPMENT
- large jar
- blotting (filter) paper
- selection of pens (not waterproof-ink pens)

Experiment steps

1 Cut a piece of blotting paper about 4 inches (10 centimeters) square. Choose two pens with the same color of ink and put a mark from each pen about 1 inch (2 centimeters) from the edge of the paper.

2 Pour 0.5 inches (1 centimeter) of water into the jar. Fold the paper into a cylinder with the spots of ink at one end. Make it smaller than the jar so that it does not touch the sides. Stand it in the water with the spots at the bottom.

3 Observe what happens. When the water has reached the top of the paper, remove the paper and allow it to dry. Now compare the two sets of separated dyes.

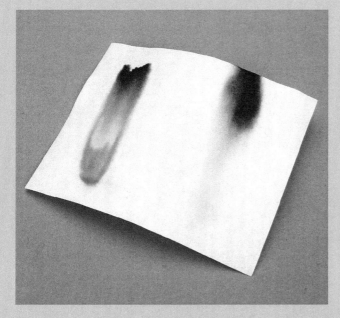

Results

Compare the two marks from the separated dyes. Are they identical? What do you think this means? You can check your results on page 47.

Evaporation

Evaporation is a method of getting a dissolved solid from a solution. You could use evaporation to extract the salt from salty water. The solution is put in a wide container so that a large area of solution is in contact with the air. The solvent gradually evaporates (in the same way a puddle dries up) and is lost into the air. The particles of the solid (or solute) do not evaporate. Eventually only the solid is left in the container.

Distillation

Distillation is a method of getting a solvent from a solution. You would use distillation if you wanted to extract the water from salty water. The solution is put in a closed flask and heated until the solvent boils to make gas. The gas flows through an attached tube into a separate container where it cools and condenses back into liquid. The solute is left in the flask.

Fractional distillation

Fractional distillation is used to separate a mixture of liquids that have different boiling points. The mixture is put in a closed flask, and is heated gradually. Each liquid in the mixture boils at a different temperature to make a gas. The gases are collected and condensed to turn them back into liquids.

Fractional distillation columns separate crude oil into gasoline, natural gas, and other useful products.

🔬 EXPERIMENT: DISTILLATION

Problem How can we purify salty water?

Hypothesis By distilling the salty water. The liquid produced should be pure water. The salt will be left behind.

EQUIPMENT
- large pan
- aluminum foil
- small bowl or dish
- ice
- salt

Experiment steps

1 Pour half an inch (1 centimeter) of water into a pan. Stir in two tablespoons of salt until the salt dissolves. Taste the water to see how salty it is. Ask an adult to help with the rest of the experiment.

2 Set a small bowl in the center of the pan. Cover the pan with aluminum foil. Gently press down the center of the foil and put some ice cubes in the dip. Make sure that the dip in the foil stays above the small bowl, but is not tightly pressed into the small bowl itself.

3 Put the pan on the stove and heat it gently. After a few minutes remove it from the heat and allow it to cool. Make sure the pan does not boil dry.

4 When the pan is cool, taste the water in the small bowl. It should be pure, unsalted water. It has evaporated from the salty water, condensed on the foil and dripped into the small bowl. The ice keeps the foil cold so that condensation happens quickly underneath the foil.

Results

What does the water taste like? Is it salty? What do you think has happened? You can check your results on page 47.

THE PERIODIC TABLE

The periodic table is a chart of all the known elements. The elements are arranged in order of their atomic numbers, but in rows, so that elements with similar properties are underneath each other. The periodic table gets its name from the fact that the elements' properties repeat themselves every few elements, or periodically. The position of an element in the periodic table gives an idea of what its properties are likely to be.

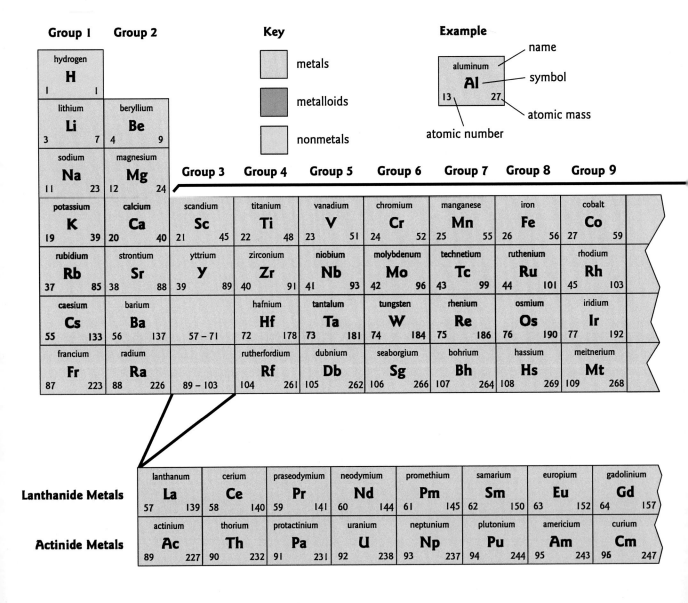

Groups and periods

The vertical columns of elements are called groups. The horizontal rows of elements are called periods. Some groups have special names:

Group 1: Alkali metals
Group 2: Alkaline earth metals
Groups 3–12: Transition metals
Group 17: Halogens
Group 18: Noble gases

The table is divided into two main sections, the metals and **nonmetals**. Between the two are elements that have some properties of metals and some of nonmetals. They are called semimetals or **metalloids**.

Group 10	Group 11	Group 12	Group 13	Group 14	Group 15	Group 16	Group 17	Group 18
								helium **He** 2 4
			boron **B** 5 11	carbon **C** 6 12	nitrogen **N** 7 14	oxygen **O** 8 16	fluorine **F** 9 19	neon **Ne** 10 20
			aluminum **Al** 13 27	silicon **Si** 14 28	phosphorus **P** 15 31	sulfur **S** 16 32	chlorine **Cl** 17 35	argon **Ar** 18 40
nickel **Ni** 28 59	copper **Cu** 29 64	zinc **Zn** 30 65	gallium **Ga** 31 70	germanium **Ge** 32 73	arsenic **As** 33 75	selenium **Se** 34 79	bromine **Br** 35 80	krypton **Kr** 36 84
palladium **Pd** 46 106	silver **Ag** 47 108	cadmium **Cd** 48 112	indium **In** 49 115	tin **Sn** 50 119	antimony **Sb** 51 122	tellurium **Te** 52 128	iodine **I** 53 127	xenon **Xe** 54 131
platinum **Pt** 78 195	gold **Au** 79 197	mercury **Hg** 80 201	thallium **Tl** 81 204	lead **Pb** 82 207	bismuth **Bi** 83 209	polonium **Po** 84 209	astatine **At** 85 210	radon **Rn** 86 222
darmstadtium **Ds** 110 281	roentgenium **Rg** 111 272	ununbium **Uub** 112 285	ununtrium **Uut** 113 284	ununquadium **Uuq** 114 289	ununpentium **Uup** 115 288	ununhexium **Uuh** 116 292		

terbium **Tb** 65 159	dysprosium **Dy** 66 163	holmium **Ho** 67 165	erbium **Er** 68 167	thulium **Tm** 69 169	ytterbium **Yb** 70 173	lutetium **Lu** 71 175
berkelium **Bk** 97 247	californium **Cf** 98 251	einsteinium **Es** 99 252	fermium **Fm** 100 257	mendelevium **Md** 101 258	nobelium **No** 102 259	lawrencium **Lr** 103 262

Common elements

Here is a table of the most common elements from the periodic table that you may come across at home or in your school's science class. The table indicates whether the element is a metal, nonmetal, or metalloid, and whether it is a solid, liquid, or gas at room temperature.

Element	Symbol	Metal or not	State at room temperature
hydrogen	H	nonmetal	gas
helium	He	nonmetal	gas
lithium	Li	metal	solid
carbon	C	nonmetal	solid
nitrogen	N	nonmetal	gas
oxygen	O	nonmetal	gas
fluorine	F	nonmetal	gas
neon	Ne	nonmetal	gas
sodium	Na	metal	solid
magnesium	Mg	metal	solid
aluminum	Al	metal	solid
silicon	Si	metalloid	solid
phosphorus	P	nonmetal	solid
sulfur	S	nonmetal	solid
chlorine	Cl	nonmetal	gas
argon	Ar	nonmetal	gas
potassium	K	metal	solid
calcium	Ca	metal	solid
iron	Fe	metal	solid
copper	Cu	metal	solid
zinc	Zn	metal	solid
bromine	Br	nonmetal	liquid
silver	Ag	metal	solid
tin	Sn	metal	solid
iodine	I	nonmetal	solid
gold	Au	metal	solid
mercury	Hg	metal	liquid
lead	Pb	metal	solid

Common chemicals

Here is a table of some common chemicals that you may come across at home or in your school's science class. The right column shows their formulas.

Gases	
hydrogen	H_2
oxygen	O_2
chlorine	Cl_2
nitrogen	N_2
carbon dioxide	CO_2
nitrogen dioxide	NO_2
Liquids and solutions	
water	H_2O
hydrochloric acid	HCl
sulfuric acid	H_2SO_4
nitric acid	HNO_3
sodium hydroxide	$NaOH$
Solids	
sodium chloride	$NaCl$
magnesium oxide	MgO
calcium carbonate	$CaCO_3$
copper sulfate	$CuSO_4$

Structures of elements and compounds

This list gives the structure of different elements and compounds. For molecules, it gives the number of atoms of each element in the molecule, and for other structures, the ratio of atoms of each element.

Name	Structure	Formula
hydrogen	molecules	H_2 (2 x H)
helium	molecules	He (1 x He)
oxygen	molecules	O_2 (2 x O)
nitrogen	molecules	N_2 (2 x N)
aluminum	metallic lattice	Al
sulfur	molecular lattice	S
chlorine	molecules	Cl_2 (2 x Cl)
water	molecules	H_2O (2 x H; 1 x O)
ammonia	molecules	NH_3 (1 x N; 3 x H)
carbon monoxide	molecules	CO (1 x C; 1 x O)
carbon dioxide	molecules	CO_2 (1 x C; 2 x O)
hydrogen sulfide	molecules	H_2S (2 x H; 1 x S)
magnesium sulfate	ionic lattice	$MgSO_4$ (1 x Mg; 1 x S; 4 x O)
sodium chloride	ionic lattice	NaCl (1 x Na; 1 x Cl)
calcium carbonate	ionic lattice	$CaCO_3$ (1 x Ca; 1 x C; 3 x O)
hydrochloric acid	ions in solution	HCl (1 x H; 1 x Cl)
sodium hydroxide	ions in solution	NaOH (1 x Na; 1 x O; 1 x H)
ethane	molecules	C_2H_6 (2 x C; 6 x H)
methane	molecules	CH_4 (1 x C; 4 x H)
glucose	molecules	$C_6H_{12}O_6$ (6 x C; 12 x H; 6 x O)

GLOSSARY OF TECHNICAL TERMS

acid liquid that can eat away metals and is neutralized by alkalis and bases. Acids have a pH below 7.

alkali liquid with a pH above 7

alloy material made by mixing a metal with another metal or a small amount of a nonmetal. For example, steel is an alloy of iron and carbon.

atom extremely tiny particles of matter. An atom is the smallest particle of an element that can exist. All substances are made up of atoms.

base any chemical that neutralizes an acid. Some bases dissolve in water to make alkalis.

boiling point temperature at which a substance changes state from liquid to gas

bond join between two atoms, ions, or molecules

cells tiny building blocks of plants and animals. All the parts of your body are made up of different types of cells, such as nerve cells and blood cells.

chemical reaction reaction that occurs when two chemicals (called the reactants) react together to form new chemicals (called the products)

compound substance that contains two or more different elements joined together by chemical bonds

condense to turn from a gas to a liquid. Gases normally condense when they cool.

conductor material that allows electricity (an electrical conductor) or heat (a heat conductor) to pass through it easily

decomposition type of chemical reaction in which a compound splits up into elements or more simple compounds

density amount of a substance (or mass) in a certain volume. Density is measured in ounces per cubic inch or pounds per cubic yard.

electrodes electrical contact that is touching a liquid in electrolysis

electrolysis method of separating a compound into its elements, using electricity

electron extremely tiny particle that is part of an atom. Electrons move around the nucleus of an atom.

element substance that contains just one type of atom. Elements are the simplest substances that exist.

extract remove from

formula collection of symbols and numbers that represents an element or compound. It shows what elements are in a compound and the ratio of the numbers of atoms of each element.

fractional distillation process of separating a mixture of liquids with different boiling points

insulator material that does not allow electricity (an electrical insulator) or heat (a heat insulator) to pass through it easily

ion type of particle. An ion is an atom that has lost or gained one or more electrons, giving it an overall positive or negative charge.

ionic compound compound made up of ions of different elements combined together

lattice structure made up of particles bonded together to form regular rows and columns

melting point temperature at which a substance changes state from solid to liquid as it warms

metal any element in the periodic table that is shiny, and that conducts electricity and heat well. Most metals are also hard.

metalloid element that cannot be classed as a metal or a nonmetal. It has some of the properties of a metal and some of the properties of a nonmetal.

microorganism living thing too small to see without a microscope

mixture substance made up of two or more elements or compounds that are not joined together by chemical bonds

molecule type of particle. A molecule is made up of two or more atoms joined together by chemical bonds. The atoms can be of the same element or different elements.

natural gas gas often found deep underground with oil or coal, which is used as a fuel. It is made up mainly of the compound methane.

neutron one of the particles that makes up the nucleus of an atom

nonmetal any element in the periodic table that is not a metal. Most nonmetals are gases.

ore material dug from the ground that contains useful elements, such as iron, aluminum, or sulfur

organic to do with living things. Organic compounds are compounds found in living things, or in the remains of living things.

oxide compound made when a metal or nonmetal combines with oxygen

particle small piece of a substance. Particles can be atoms, ions, molecules, or groups made up of atoms, ions, or molecules joined together.

photosynthesis chemical reaction in which plants make food from water and carbon dioxide using the energy in sunlight

properties characteristics of a substance, such as its strength, melting point, and density

proton one of the particles that makes up the nucleus of an atom

reactant chemical that takes part in a chemical reaction

reactivity series list of common metals, arranged in order of how quickly they react with other substances, such as acids, water, and air. The most reactive metals are at the top.

respiration chemical reaction in which animals and plants release energy from food

solute substance that dissolves in a solvent to make a solution

solution substance made when a solid, gas, or liquid dissolves in a liquid

solvent liquid that a substance dissolves in to make a solution

symbol single letter or two letters used to represent an element in chemical formulas and equations

unique only one

FURTHER READING

e. science encyclopedia. New York: DK Publishing, 2004.

Miller, Ron. *The Elements.* Minneapolis, Minn.: Twenty-First Century Books, 2006.

Parsons, Jayne. *The Way Science Works.* New York: DK Publishing, 2002.

Solway, Andrew. *A History of Super Science: Atoms and Elements.* Chicago: Heinemann Raintree, 2006.

Useful websites

http://www.chemicool.com
All you ever needed to know about the elements — and more!

http://www.chemicalelements.com
An interactive Periodic table. Originally created, in 1996, as an 8th grade science project.

http://www.creative-chemistry.org.uk
An interactive chemistry site including fun practical activities, worksheets, quizzes, puzzles, and more!

http://www.heinemannexplore.com
An online resource for school libraries and classrooms containing articles, investigations, biographies, and activities related to all areas of the science curriculum.

http://www.webelements.com/webelements/scholar

The Periodic table – online! Discover more about all the elements and their properties.

Experiment results

page 15: Zinc fizzes most quickly, so it must be the most reactive of the three metals. Iron fizzes a little bit, and copper does not fizz at all. It is the least reactive.

page 17: The gas that forms on the pencil lead should smell a little like a swimming pool. It is chlorine gas, formed by electrolysis of the salt (sodium chloride) solution.

page 27: When you crumble the burned aluminum you should see a gray powder. This is aluminum oxide. When the metal burns in the flame, the outer layer of the aluminum combines with oxygen to make this compound.

page 37: If the patterns of dyes on the paper for each ink match, it is likely that the two inks are from the same manufacturer.

page 39: The water in the small bowl should be pure, unsalted water. It has evaporated from the salty water, condensed on the foil, and dripped into the small bowl. The ice keeps the foil cold so that condensation happens quickly. You have successfully used distillation to separate pure water (the solvent) from the salt solution.

INDEX